THE

SLOW COOKER COOK BOOK

FOR KIDS

20 SIMPLE KID-FRIENDLY RECIPES

GRACE ISABELLE

TABLE OF CONTENTS

INTRODUCTION

Welcome to "The Slow Cooker Cookbook for Kids: 20 Easy Kid-Friendly Recipes," a culinary adventure created to help your young chefs learn and love cooking. We've carefully chosen simple-to-follow recipes in this lovely book to introduce young cooks to the technique of slow cooking. As parents, we know how important it is to inculcate good eating habits in our children at a young age, and the slow cooker is the ideal ally in accomplishing this. It makes cooking easier, but it also lets kids experiment with different tastes and sensations. With its clear instructions, this cookbook encourages young cooks to be independent in the kitchen and develop their creativity and confidence. Together, let's go on a delicious journey filled with memories and wholesome food!

DELICIOUS SLOW COOKER RECIPES FOR KIDS

1. Cheesy Tacos with Chicken:

Ingredients:

Skinless, bony chicken breasts

Taco Seasoning, 2 tablespoons

Green chilies and diced tomatoes (10 ounce can)

Green Chiles, diced (4 ounce can)

15 oz. of salsa

Dim Sum Tortillas

Toppers for Tacos

Preparation:

In a crock pot, combine the chicken, taco seasoning, diced tomatoes, and diced green chilies.

Cook on high for 3–4 hours, or cover and cook slowly on low for 6–8 hours.

Add the salsa after shredding the chicken.

The cheese should be well cooked after 15 to 20 minutes of gentle cooking under cover.

Transfer into taco shells and accompany with your family's favorite taco fixings, such as lettuce, tomato, sour cream, and black olives.

2. Mac 'n' Cheese

Ingredients

1 packet (16 ounces) of elbow macaroni

Half a cup of butter

To taste, add salt and ground black pepper.

1 package (16 ounces) of shredded cheddar cheese

1 5-oz can of evaporated milk

2 eggs, whisked thoroughly

2 cups of whole milk

1 (11-oz) can of condensed cheddar cheese

Pinch of paprika, or more, to taste (Optional)

Preparation:

Bring a big saucepan of water that has been lightly salted to a rolling boil.

Add the macaroni and bring it back to a boil.

Cook pasta uncovered for about 8 minutes, stirring periodically, until it's firm to the bite but still tender. After draining, put the pasta in a slow cooker.

Stir the butter into the pasta and add salt and pepper to taste.

Over the Pasta sprinkle half of the Cheddar cheese and mix.

Combine eggs and evaporated milk in a bowl and whisk until smooth; incorporate into pasta mixture.

In a bowl, whisk together milk and condensed soup until smooth; add into pasta mixture.

Over the pasta mixture, sprinkle the remaining cheese and add the paprika.

Cook on Low for 3 hours, watching after 2 hours 30 minutes to make sure the edges are not getting too brown.

3. Sloppy Joe Sliders:

Ingredients:

1 pound Ground beef

1 chopped yellow onion

1 chopped bell pepper, green or red

1 cup of ketchup

8 ounces Tomato sauce cans

2 Tbsp. mustard

1 teaspoon vinegar made from apples

1 teaspoon Sauce from Worcestershire

3/4 teaspoon salt

1/4 teaspoon chili

1/4 teaspoon minced garlic

1/4 teaspoon spice mix

1 tablespoon browned sugar

Preparation:

Place a large skillet over medium-high heat on the stovetop.

Add the ground beef, onion, and bell pepper to the heated pan. Crumble and brown the steak. If your ground beef is too fatty, drain your meat.

To the slow cooker, add the beef, onion, and bell pepper. Stir in the remaining

Stir. Put the slow cooker's lid on.

Cook on low for 3 hours or high for 2.

Watch the beef mixture closely, and stir if it appears to be burning on the edges.

Top the toasted buns with a mountain of Sloppy Joe meat.

If desired, garnish with pickles and cheese.

4. Stew made with chicken and vegetables

Ingredients:

2 breasts of chicken

1 chopped onion

2 celery stalks, chopped

4 carrots into rounds after peeling them.

2 medium russet potatoes into small, bite-sized pieces.

1 bay leaf

2 tsp salt

1 tsp finely chopped garlic

½ teaspoon dried thyme

½ teaspoon seasoning

4 cups of low-sodium chicken stock or broth

2 tablespoons of cornstarch and 2 tablespoons of cold water

1 tablespoon of parsley, chopped for the garnish

Preparation:

With the exception of the corn starch, add everything to the crock pot.

Cook the chicken for 6 to 8 hours on low, or until it is tender.

Cut the chicken into shreds.

In the meantime, mix the water and corn starch in a cup.

Pour into the slow cooker. Add the chicken and stir.

After 30 more minutes of cooking, garnish with fresh parsley and serve.

5. BBQ pulled pork sandwiches

Ingredients:

RUB

2 tablespoons of brown sugar

2 teaspoons of paprika powder

1 teaspoon of onion powder

1 teaspoon of garlic powder

½ tsp cumin powder

3/4 teaspoon powdered mustard

1 teaspoon of salt

A half-tsp black pepper

Pork

Pork shoulder weighing 1.5–2.2 kg/3–4.5 pound

1 ½cups apple juice or cider

Small amount of cole slaw

Between 6 and 8 bread rolls

Grilled sauce

1 cup of cooked pork slow cooker juices

2½ cups ketchup

½ cup of vinegar made from apple cider

2 cups brown sugar

1½ teaspoons of each of mustard powder, onion powder, and black pepper

1 tablespoon of lemon juice

1 tablespoon Worcestershire sauce

Preparation:

Combine the rub and rub the mixture all over the pork. Marinate for 1 hour, if desired.

Cover with apple cider and set in a slow cooker.

Cook on low for 8 hours or on high pressure for 1 hour and 30 minutes.

Scrape pork off liquid and place in roasting pan.

OPTION: Roast the pork at 180C/350F for 20 to 30 minutes, or until browned.

Prepare the BBQ sauce.

Using forks, shred pork

Add BBQ sauce.

Pile pulled pork onto warm bread and cover with Cole slaw to make pulled pork sandwiches.

6. Veggie-Packed Chili

Ingredients:

1 cup chopped onions, either red or yellow, around ½ large

1 large carrot and 1 cup of sliced carrot

1 medium red bell pepper, thinly sliced and seeded

3 minced garlic cloves

1 cup of corn kernels, frozen

14 ounces of washed and drained canned pinto beans

14 ounces of rinsed and drained canned black beans

1 cup dry lentils, either brown or green

28 ounces of fire-roasted or normal tomatoes in a can

4 cups of broth made with vegetables

2 tsp kosher salt, or according to taste

1 and a half tsp chili powder

1 teaspoon paprika

1-half teaspoon of cumin

1 tablespoon of olive oil

1½ lime, or 1 tablespoon of lime juice

Add extra chopped fresh cilantro for garnish (optional), and use ¼ cup of it.

Preparation:

Fill a 6 to 8-quart slow cooker with all the ingredients, from the onion to the olive oil. Mix everything together.

Cook with a lid on for 7 to 8 hours on Low or 5 to 6 hours on High.

Stir in the chopped cilantro, if using, and lime juice once the cooking time is complete and the lentils and carrots are soft. If necessary, add more salt after tasting.

Spoon chili into bowls and garnish with additional cilantro and desired toppings.

7. Sweet and Sour Meatballs

Ingredients:

2 pounds of ground beef

2 eggs

½ cup of breadcrumbs

1/4 cup finely chopped onions

1 tsp salt

½ teaspoon of pepper

½ teaspoon of powdered garlic

1 (12-oz) bottle of chili sauce

1½ cups grape jelly

2 tsp of parsley

Cooking oil

Preparation:

Set the broiler to high. Apply cooking spray to the foil that lines a sheet pan.

In a large bowl, combine the ground beef, eggs, breadcrumbs, onion, salt, pepper, and garlic powder. Mix well until well blended.

After forming the beef mixture into 1-inch meatballs, arrange them on the pan that has been ready.

Broil until golden brown, 8 to 10 minutes.

Make the sauce while the meatballs are cooking. Melt the grape jelly in a saucepan over medium heat or in the microwave in 30-second increments.

Stir in the chili sauce once the jelly has melted.

Apply some cooking spray to a slow cooker. Pour the sauce over the meatballs after adding them. Toss in the coat.

Cook on low for 3 hours. After adding the parsley, serve.

8. Teriyaki Chicken Bowls

Ingredients

1 and a half pounds of chicken breasts

2 tsp finely chopped garlic

2 tsp finely chopped ginger

1/4 cup of honey

3 tsp of brown sugar

1/2 cup soy sauce reduced in sodium

A couple of tsp of toasted sesame oil

2 tsp of rice vinegar

1/4 cup of cold water

2 tsp cornstarch

1 spoonful of seeds from sesame

2 tsp finely chopped green onion

Preparation:

Put the breasts of chicken in the slow cooker.

Mix the rice vinegar, sesame oil, brown sugar, ginger, garlic, and honey in a small bowl.

Cover the chicken with the soy sauce mixture.

Place a cover on and cook for 3–4 hours on high or 6–7 hours on low.

Using forks, shred the chicken after taking it out of the slow cooker.

Using a colander, transfer the teriyaki sauce from the slow cooker into a saucepan. After setting the pot on medium-high heat, bring it to a simmer.

Stir the cornstarch and water in a small bowl until the cornstarch is dissolved.

After adding the cornstarch to the pan, bring it to a boil. Cook until sauce has slightly thickened, 1 to 2 minutes.

After adding the sauce, mix the shredded chicken to coat it.

Serve after sprinkling with sesame seeds and green onions.

9. Pizza pasta casserole

Ingredients:

1 ½ pounds of ground beef

1 sliced medium onion

15 ounces of tomato sauce

14 ounces of pizza sauce

2 tablespoons of tomato paste

3 cups of pasta in spiral shape

2 (3.5-ounce) packages of pepperoni slices each

2 cups of mozzarella cheese, shredded

Preparation:

Cook the beef and onion over medium heat until the meat is no longer pink. Then drain. Add tomato paste, pizza sauce, and tomato sauce and stir.

In the meantime, prepare pasta as directed on the package.

Arrange a third of the spaghetti, meat mixture, pepperoni, and cheese in a 5 quart slow cooker. Continue twice more, concluding with cheese. Once heated through, cover and simmer on low for 3 to 4 hours.

10. Chicken noodle soup

Ingredients:

1 to 1½ pounds of chicken breasts

1 big sliced yellow onion

3 big carrots cut into coins after being peeled

2 celery stalks, cut

3–4 minced garlic cloves

½ teaspoon dried thyme

½ teaspoon dried rosemary

½ teaspoon of kosher salt

¼ teaspoon black pepper

1 bay leaf, if desired

2 tsp of chicken base

8 to 9 cups of low-sodium chicken broth

8 ounces of extra-large or wide egg noodles

Minced fresh parsley (for garnish)

Preparation:

Add trimmed chicken breasts to the bottom of a 6-quart or larger slow cooker. Sprinkle salt, pepper, dried thyme, dried rosemary, onion, carrots, celery, garlic, and, if desired, a bay leaf on top.

Place a dollop of chicken base on top and cover with chicken broth. Stir gently to mix. Cook with a lid on for 6–8 hours on low or 3–4 hours on high.

Take the chicken out of the slow cooker and place it in a big mixing dish. Cut up chicken. After discarding the bay leaf, put the shredded chicken back in the slow cooker.

Cook egg noodles al dente as directed on the packet.

To enable the flavors to meld, add the egg noodles to the soup and cook on low for 5 minutes.

Garnish with finely chopped fresh parsley and a dash of black pepper.

11. Apple Sauce Chicken

Ingredients:

6 whole chicken breasts

⅔ cup Applesauce

⅔ cup of your preferred brand of barbecue sauce

2 teaspoons of either light or dark brown sugar

1/4 tsp finely ground black pepper

1 tsp ground chili powder

Preparation:

Use nonstick cooking spray or line a 6-quart slow cooker with a slow cooker liner.

The chicken breasts should be placed in the crock's bottom.

Combine the other ingredients (applesauce, chili powder, brown sugar, black pepper, and barbecue sauce) in a small bowl, then drizzle the mixture over the chicken.

Once the chicken reaches a temperature of 165° F on a meat thermometer, cover and simmer on low for 4 to 6 hours.

12. Mini Meat ball subs

Ingredients:

1 pound of lean ground beef

½ cup of dried breadcrumbs

1/4–1/2 teaspoon onion powder or 2 tablespoons of coarsely minced onions

1 teaspoon of salt

Spoonful of Worcestershire sauce

1 egg

1 tablespoon of grated Parmesan cheese

1 32-oz container of spaghetti sauce

6 to 8 hoagie rolls or 6 to 8 hot dog buns

Cheese mozzarella (sliced or shredded)

Preparation:

In a large bowl, combine the first 7 ingredients. Using your hands, fully combine just until blended. Form into about thirty 1-inch balls.

Bake for 20 to 25 minutes at 400°F in an ungreased rectangular pan (13 by 9 by 2), or until light brown. Alternatively, cook meatballs in a baking dish without oil for 6 minutes on High, flipping once. Alternatively, sauté in a frying pan over medium heat for about 20 minutes, rotating regularly, until golden.

Put the spaghetti sauce and cooked meatballs into the crock cooker. Simmer for roughly 2 hours on low. Stir every hour or so if you cook for a longer time.

Top the meatballs and sauce with mozzarella cheese and place them inside buns or rolls.

13. Creamy Tomato Basil Soup

Ingredients:

3 medium-sized carrots, chopped and skinned.

1 medium yellow onion, chopped coarsely.

3 ribs of coarsely diced celery

28 ounces of chopped tomatoes in a can (with liquid)

1 teaspoon dried or 1 tablespoon chopped fresh oregano

¼ cup chopped fresh basil or 1 tablespoon dried

Triple-Cup Vegetable Stock

Grated Parmesan Cheese, 1 cup

2 cups half-and-half (fat-free optional)

Add pepper and salt (to taste)

Preparation:

Add the carrots, onion, celery, canned tomatoes, oregano, basil, and vegetable broth to a 4- to 6-quart slow cooker.

Vegetables should be cooked and tender after 6 to 8 hours of low cooking under cover.

Right inside the slow cooker, use a hand-held blender to mix the soup until it reaches your preferred smoothness.

Increase the heat to high and stir in the half-and-half and grated Parmesan cheese for the soup in the crock-pot.

1 cup of grated Parmesan cheese and 2 cups of half-and-half

Once the soup is heated, cover and continue cooking for a further 30 to 40 minutes.

After tasting the soup, adjust the seasoning with salt and pepper to taste and serve.

14. Teriyaki Meatballs Skewers

Ingredients:

1 packet of 32-ounce frozen meatballs

1 (14-ounce) jar Teriyaki Sauce

1 (20-oz) can of pineapple pieces or nibbles in juice

Preparation:

To a big skillet, add the meatballs and teriyaki sauce. The meatballs work best when they are all in 1 layer.

Save the juice from the drained pineapple.

Toss the meatballs in the skillet with the pineapple and 1/4 cup of the conserved liquid. Mix everything together.

Cook the meatballs, covered, over medium heat for about 20 to 25 minutes, stirring periodically, or until they are hot and well warmed through.

Serve with rice and vegetables for a supper. Meatballs with pineapple pieces on skewers can be served hot as an appetizer.

In the Slow Cooker

Spoon nonstick cooking spray onto the liner of a slow cooker and add meatballs and teriyaki sauce. Save the juice from the drained pineapple. Toss the meatballs in the skillet with the pineapple and 1/4 cup of the conserved liquid. Mix everything together.

Cook until heated, about 3–4 hours on low.

Serve with rice and vegetables for a supper.

15. Cheesy potato casserole

Ingredients:

1 (2 pound) box of thawed frozen Southern-style hash brown potatoes

4 cups of cheddar cheese, shredded

2 (10.5-oz) condensed cream of chicken soup cans

1 (8-oz) carton of sour cream

1 cup chopped yellow onion (Optional)

1 cup of milk

1 tsp finely chopped garlic

1 cup of crumbled Cheese-It or other cheese-flavored crackers, split

Preparation:

In a slow cooker, combine hash brown potatoes, condensed soup, sour cream, onion, milk, seasoned salt, garlic, and half a cup of cheese-flavored crackers.

Simmer on Low for about 3 hours, stirring now and then, or until well cooked.

Add the remaining 1/2 cup of cheese-flavored crackers on top after stirring.

16. Honey Garlic Chicken Drumsticks

Ingredients:

3 pounds of chicken thighs or legs

2 tspn of kosher salt

½ teaspoon Pepper

1/4 cup water

½ cup Honey

⅓ cup low-sodium soy sauce

2 Tablespoons Ketchup

1 tsp grated ginger

4–5 of crushed or finely chopped garlic cloves

2 tablespoons of coarsely chopped onion

1/4–1/2 tsp red pepper flakes

To thicken (mix together)

Corn starch, 2 tablespoons

3 Tablespoons of Cold Water

Preparation:

Mist the crock's interior. Activate using the Low setting.

Coat the chicken in salt and pepper on all sides.

After adding the water to the crock, add the chicken to it.
Put the lid on to allow the heat to begin.

Combine the ketchup, honey, soy sauce, ginger, garlic, onion, and red pepper flakes in a 2-cup measuring cup. Cover the chicken with the liquid.

Cook for 2 to 4 hours on low; check after 2 hours. The size of the chicken and/or the brand of slow cooker you own may affect the cooking time.

Transfer the chicken to a platter and cover it loosely. Preheat the slow cooker on high.

Mix the cold water and corn starch with a whisk. Stir in addition to the liquid in the crock.

Return the chicken to the crock and cook it on High for 10 to 15 minutes, or until the internal temperature reaches 165° F.

Serve with cooked rice and top with cilantro, scallions, or sesame seeds.

17. *Vegetarian Sloppy Joes*

Ingredients:

1 cup of carrots, chopped finely

1 cup of finely chopped mushrooms

1 cup of finely chopped onions

2 minced garlic cloves

½ cup of brown lentils

½ cup of quinoa

1 8-oz can of tomato sauce

2 tsp pure maple syrup

2 tsp spicy sauce

2 tsp of mustard

1 tablespoon of powdered chilies

1 tsp of paprika

Pinch of salt & pepper

3–4 cups vegetables broth

Preparation:

Starting with 3 cups of broth, add everything to the slow cooker. Combine, cover, and adjust to high. Cook for 2–3 hours on high, or 4–6 hours on low. When necessary, check and add extra liquid.

Serve hot inside a spaghetti squash or on a bread or biscuit

18. Beef and Vegetable Stir-Fry

Ingredients:

2 tsp of vegetable oil

1 pound of 2-inch-long strips of beef sirloin

⅓ Cup of raw broccoli florets

1 red bell pepper, sliced into sticks

2 carrots, cut thinly

1 sliced green onion

1 tsp finely chopped garlic

2 tsp soy sauce

2 tablespoons of toasted sesame seeds

Preparation:

Apply nonstick cooking spray to a slow cooker before using it.

To prepare the beef, put the chopped strips in a freezer bag with a zip-top and add the cornstarch. After giving the steak a good toss to ensure even coating, place it in the slow cooker.

In a small bowl, combine the brown sugar, soy sauce, sesame oil, ginger, garlic, red pepper, and black pepper to make the sauce. Cover the beef with the mixture.

Arrange the vegetables on top of the steak and add salt to taste.

Once the vegetables are soft, simmer them on low for 4 to 6 hours with a cover on.

Serve the steak and veggies over noodles or rice after tossing them together. Add sliced green onions as a garnish.

19. Buffalo Chicken Wraps

Ingredients:

2 tablespoons ranch seasoning blend

1 teaspoon of cayenne

2 pounds chicken breasts

1 cup of buffalo sauce

Preparation:

In a small dish, whisk together the cayenne pepper and ranch seasoning blend.

After rubbing the chicken breasts with the spice mixture, put them in a slow cooker.

Dredge in ¾ cup buffalo sauce.

Cook slowly for 3–4 hours on high or 6–8 hours on low.

After taking off the slow cooker's lid, shred the chicken within with 2 forks.

Toss to mix in the remaining ¼ cup of buffalo sauce in the slow cooker.

20. Cinnamon Apple Oatmeal

Ingredients:

1 Cup Oats, Steel-Cut

2 teaspoons of cinnamon

1 chopped apple

1/4 cup raisins (optional)

To taste, stevia or sugar

Preparation:

Add raisins, cinnamon, and diced apples to the slow cooker.

Pour in 1 cup of instant oats.

Fill the slow cooker with the 4 cups of liquid.

Cook for 7 hours on low with a cover on.

CONCLUSION

As we come to the end of "The Slow Cooker Cookbook for Kids," I hope these 20 simple and kid-friendly recipes have awakened your child's love of cooking in addition to satisfying your palate. We've discovered the delight of cooking delectable meals together through this culinary journey, and it has encouraged a love of healthful ingredients and creative cooking. The slow cooker is an excellent teaching tool for kids to start cooking because of its ease of use and safety features. Recall that the kitchen is a space for learning, sharing stories, and developing relationships as you continue to play with flavors and textures. I hope the knowledge gained and the experiences created in these pages stick with your family and inspire a lifetime of food adventures and quality time spent at the dinner table.

Have fun in the kitchen!

Made in United States
Orlando, FL
03 May 2025

61014162R00017